A Teacher's Guide to The Boy in the Striped Pajamas

A Teacher's Guide to The Boy in the Striped Pajamas

By Greg Slingerland

Upper Canada Press

First Printing: 2015

ISBN 978-1-329-73936-9

Upper Canada Press
St. Catharines, Ontario, Canada

All quotation from *The Boy in the Striped Pajamas* are taken from:

Boyne, John. *The Boy in the Striped Pajamas*. David Fickling Books, 2006, New York.

Before Reading...

- Take a look at the front and back cover of *The Boy in the Striped Pajamas*. What observations can you make about the book?

    o What do you think the book will be about?

    o What genre do you think the book is? (i.e. science fiction)

- Can you judge a book by its cover?

- How do you choose a book and decide if it's worth reading?

- Who is the author of *The Boy in the Striped Pajamas*?

- Poll – Have students walk to different marked out spots in the classroom. Students answer the poll question by going to a spot in the room with a sign saying 'strongly agree', a spot that says 'maybe', or a spot that says 'strongly disagree'. Have the students listen carefully before moving.

    o Do you like exploring?

    o Did you/do you have an active imagination? What kinds of things captivated your imagination?

    o If you came home from school and your parents told you that you were moving to a new home in a different part of the country, how would you feel? Would you be excited?

Chapter One – Bruno Makes a Discovery

1. Who is Maria? Why does she never look up from the carpet?

_____

_____

_____

_____

2. How is Maria treated by the family?

_____

_____

_____

_____

3. Why were the rims of Mother's eyes red?

_____

_____

_____

_____

4. Who was the 'Hopeless Case'?

_____

_____

_____

_____

5. How did Bruno know his father had an important job?

_____

_____

_____

_____

_____

6. Describe Bruno's character.

_____

_____

_____

_____

7. Look up the word naïve. Does this describe Bruno? Why or why not?

_____

_____

_____

8. What can we piece together about the setting so far?

_____

_____

_____

_____

_____

_____

_____

_____

Chapter One – Bruno Makes a Discovery

Answers

1. Who is Maria? Why does she never look up from the carpet?
   a. Maria is the family maid.
   b. Maria is in a lower class and she does not look the family members in the eye. She is not equal.
2. How is Maria treated by the family?
   a. Bruno doesn't yet understand Maria's position as a servant and treats her quite well – as a member of the family. Mother treats Maria politely but Father treats Maria rudely.
3. Why were the rims of Mother's eyes red?
   a. Mother's eyes were red because she was crying and upset about having to move out of their beautiful home in Berlin.
4. Who was the 'Hopeless Case'?
   a. Bruno's sister Gretel.
5. How did Bruno know his father had an important job?
   a. Bruno could tell by the visitors that came to the house. The men had fancy uniforms and the women came in with typewriters. People always talked about how the Fury (the Fuehrer, Adolf Hitler) had big things in mind for Father.
6. Describe Bruno's character.
   a. Bruno was innocent (had no idea what was happening around him), private (kept things at the back of his closet), ambitious (had big plans), friendly, stubborn, and had an active imagination.
7. Look up the word naive. Does this describe Bruno? Why or why not?
   a. Showing a lack of experience, judgment, or wisdom. Gullible.
8. What can we piece together about the setting so far?
   a. Berlin, men with uniforms, the Fuehrer, war-time (lights-out at night).

Chapter Two – The New House

Find as many comparisons as you can between the new house and the house in Berlin.

The New House	The House in Berlin

1. What was Bruno's solution to the 'bad situation' at the new house?

_____

_____

_____

2. What happened in Bruno's room that "made him feel very cold and unsafe"?

_____

_____

_____

Chapter Two – The New House

<table>
<tr><td colspan="2">Find as many comparisons as you can between the new house and the house in Berlin.</td></tr>
<tr><th>The New House</th><th>The House in Berlin</th></tr>
<tr><td>Stood all on its own, desolate</td><td>Quiet street, big houses around</td></tr>
<tr><td>No other boys to play with – neither friends nor trouble</td><td>Other boys in the neighbouring houses</td></tr>
<tr><td>Only three floor house – nothing to explore</td><td>Enormous house</td></tr>
<tr><td>No other streets around the new house</td><td>The neighbourhood was a busy and happy place; markets</td></tr>
<tr><td>No cafes and no laughter</td><td>Sidewalk cafes/bars; laughter</td></tr>
<tr><td>Maria and "three others who were quite skinny"</td><td>Maria and Berlin staff</td></tr>
</table>

1. What was Bruno's solution to the 'bad situation' at the new house?

   "I think you should just tell Father that you've changed your mind and, well, if we have to stay here for the rest of the day and have dinner here this evening and sleep here tonight because we're all tired, then that's all right, but we should probably get up early in the morning if we're to make it back to Berlin by tea-time tomorrow."

2. What happened in Bruno's room that "made him feel very cold and unsafe"?

   A window that he hoped he could see a scene similar to his neighbourhood back in Berlin. The sight out the window, however, made him feel uncomfortable.

Chapter Three – The Hopeless Case

Name: _____

We get to know Gretel, also known as 'The Hopeless Case', in this chapter. So far, we have been looking at this story only through Bruno's eyes. How do you think Gretel feels about the move and the new home? Do you think she understands the situation better than Bruno? Write two diary entries from Gretel's perspective. The first diary entry should be about moving away from Berlin, and the second diary entry should be about her impressions of the new home.

Dear Diary,

_____

_____

_____

_____

_____

_____

_____

_____

_____

_____

_____

_____

_____

Dear Diary,

_____

_____

_____

_____

_____

_____

_____

_____

_____

_____

_____

_____

Chapter Four – What They Saw Through the Window

1. What was Gretel's explanation for the scene outside of Bruno's window?

_____

_____

_____

_____

_____

_____

2. What were all of the people behind the fences wearing?

_____

_____

_____

_____

3. Based on what you know so far about the story, what do you think is happening outside of Bruno's window?

_____

_____

_____

_____

_____

_____

4. Based on what we know about Bruno so far (e.g. he likes to explore), what predictions can you make about what is going to happen in the next few chapters?

_____

_____

_____

_____

_____

Name: _____

Chapter 4

Picture yourself standing in front of window alongside of Gretel and Bruno. Draw the scene you would see from the window. Be sure to include the following in the picture: garden, bench with plaque, wire fences, huts, buildings with smoke stacks, and people in striped pajamas.

Chapter Four – What They Saw Through the Window

1. What was Gretel's explanation for the scene outside of Bruno's window?
   a. Gretel explains that the people and the buildings must indicate that they are in the countryside.

2. What were all of the people behind the fences wearing?
   a. Striped pajamas, or concentration camp uniforms. These were threadbare, striped uniforms with matching caps. An identifying badge was sewn on the front or prisoners had armbands.

3. Based on what you know so far about the story, what do you think is happening outside of Bruno's window?
   a. Bruno and Gretel were the seeing the work camp section of Auschwitz-Birkenau. They could see the chimneys from the crematorium in the far off distance.

4. Based on what we know about Bruno so far (e.g. he likes to explore), what predictions can you make about what is going to happen in the next few chapters?

Chapter Five – Out Of Bounds At All Time And No Exceptions

1. What did Bruno's mother mistakenly admit in front of Maria?

_____

_____

_____

_____

2. Bruno reflects on his trip from Berlin and his time at the railway station. Why do you think the railway station was so crowded?

_____

_____

_____

_____

3. "His thick dark hair [Bruno's father] had obviously been recently lacquered and combed, and as Bruno watched from above he felt both scared and in awe of him." What kind of a relationship did Bruno have with his Father? Was this a normal relationship? Use some other examples to back up your explanation.

_____

_____

_____

_____

_____

4. How was Father's office different than the rest of the house?

_____

_____

_____

_____

5. Bruno asked his father who the people in the huts were – the people who were all dressed the same. What was his father's answer?

_____

_____

_____

_____

_____

6. What did Bruno think *Heil Hitler* meant? What did it really mean?

_____

_____

_____

_____

Setting

We learn a lot about the setting of *The Boy in the Striped Pajamas* in this chapter. Piece together all of the clues given in this chapter by writing a descriptive paragraph about the setting of this novel. You may need to do some research to help you. Use the following points and questions to help you with writing your paragraph:

- Who is the Fury?
- What is Out-With? What is the proper name? What was the place used for?
- People in the huts with the striped pajamas
- Heil Hitler
- Men in uniforms

Chapter Five – Out Of Bounds At All Time And No Exceptions

Answers

1. What did Bruno's mother mistakenly admit in front of Maria?

    a. Bruno's mother exclaims that they should never have hosted the Fury, or Hitler, for dinner. She also criticized her husband's ambitions to get ahead. She's angry that her husband is not putting his family before his country.

2. Bruno reflects on his trip from Berlin and his time at the railway station. Why do you think the railway station was so crowded?

    a. While Bruno's train had plenty of space, the train across from the platform, which was headed in the same direction, was packed. This train was (assumedly) transporting Jews to the East, or to Auschwitz.

3. "His thick dark hair [Bruno's father] had obviously been recently lacquered and combed, and as Bruno watched from above he felt both scared and in awe of him." What kind of a relationship did Bruno have with his Father? Was this a normal relationship? Use some other examples to back up your explanation.

    a. Bruno's relationship with his Father is very formal, as if Bruno is another one of his father's soldiers. Father expects Bruno to obey without question and to salute like a soldier. He also thinks that Bruno should be impressed, like his soldiers are, by his high-ranking uniform and at having the ear of the Fuhrer. In reality, Bruno thinks that Hitler is an angry man and that his father made a big mistake by moving the family out to Auschwitz. The uniforms do not impress Bruno but scare him, as does his father's manner around the household.

4. How was Father's office different than the rest of the house?

    a. The office is plush and well furnished. It is the most important part of the house. It fits in with the theme that the family has been given a backseat. Father's career is the most important thing in the family's life and all else is secondary.

5. Bruno asked his father who the people in the huts were – the people who were all dressed the same. What was his father's answer?

   a. Bruno's father is a little thrown off by the question at first, and struggles to answer the question. He tells Bruno that they are not really people, but cannot explain to Bruno why. Bruno's innocence is a barrier to understanding the Nazi doctrine of the *Untermensch* (inferior races). To some extent, Father does not want to ruin Bruno's innocence.

6. What did Bruno think *Heil Hitler* meant? What did it really mean?

   a. Bruno thinks it means "Well, goodbye for now, have a pleasant afternoon."

   b. Adolf Hitler, who claims to have started the salute, wrote:

   "I made it the salute of the Party long after the Duce had adopted it. I'd read the description of the sitting of the Diet of Worms, in the course of which Luther was greeted with the German salute. It was to show him that he was not being confronted with arms, but with peaceful intentions. In the days of Frederick the Great, people still saluted with their hats, with pompous gestures. In the Middle Ages the serfs humbly doffed their bonnets, whilst the noblemen gave the German salute. It was in the Ratskeller at Bremen, about the year 1921, that I first saw this style of salute. It must be regarded as a survival of an ancient custom, which originally signified: "See, I have no weapon in my hand!" I introduced the salute into the Party at our first meeting in Weimar. The SS at once gave it a soldierly style. It's from that moment that our opponents honored us with the epithet "dogs of Fascists".

Chapter Six – The Overpaid Maid

1. Why does Maria scold Bruno for saying "Stupid Father"? Why does she say that his father is a good man?

   _____

   _____

   _____

   _____

   _____

   _____

   _____

2. Does Maria's account of how Bruno's father helped her change how you see Bruno's Father? Explain.

   _____

   _____

   _____

   _____

   _____

3. What is Maria's advice to Bruno?

   _____

   _____

   _____

4. How does Gretel treat Maria? How is this different from Bruno's view of Maria?

   _____

   _____

   _____

   _____

Chapter Six – The Overpaid Maid

Answers

1. Why does Maria scold Bruno for saying "Stupid Father"? Why does she say that his father is a good man?
   a. Father is taking care of the family and family staff
   b. Maria tells Bruno how Father has helped her. He gave Maria a job, home and food. He also took care of her ailing mother and paid for the medical bills.

2. Does Maria's account of how Bruno's father helped her change how you see Bruno's Father? Explain.
   a. Various
   b. Bruno's father has changed along with all of Germany. Germany used to be a compassionate place and a place full of laughter. Now the Germans, Father included, are preparing for war. Worse still, Father has bought into the Nazi doctrine that the Aryan race is superior. The staff don't dare look Father in the eye and bow their heads. Father now thinks Maria is overpaid – especially now that he can have Jewish slaves from Auschwitz for free.

3. What is Maria's advice to Bruno?
   a. Maria tells Bruno to keep quiet – to keep his opinions to himself. His opinions could get the household and family into trouble. She tells him to stay quiet and focus on his schoolwork. Maria also tells him to obey his father – no matter what.

4. How does Gretel treat Maria? How is this different from Bruno's view of Maria?
   a. Gretel treats Maria as inferior. She is buying into her father's view of class hierarchy. She doesn't see Maria as a person, but as a maid. That's the only reason for Maria's existence. Bruno on the other hand, see Maria as part of the family.

Chapter Seven – How Mother Took Credit for Something That She Hadn't Done

1. Who was Herr Roller?

_____

_____

_____

_____

_____

2. Why didn't Bruno like Lieutenant Kotler?

_____

_____

_____

_____

_____

3. What do we learn about Pavel, the family's waiter?

_____

_____

_____

_____

4. Explain the title of the chapter.

_____

_____

_____

_____

_____

Chapter Seven – How Mother Took Credit for Something That She Hadn't Done

Answers

1. Who was Herr Roller?

    a. A former WWI veteran who was suffering from the effects of a head injury from the war and PTSD from the trenches. Herr Roller fought alongside Bruno's father.

2. Why didn't Bruno like Lieutenant Kotler?

    a. Lieutenant Kotler called Bruno "little man" which was demeaning. He ruffled his hair as if he was a young child. He flirted with Gretel.

3. What do we learn about Pavel, the family's waiter?

    a. Pavel is a Jewish prisoner in Auschwitz. He was once a doctor before being arrested by the Nazis.

4. Explain the title of the chapter.

    a. Mother doesn't want the Commandant, her husband, to know that a Jew cleaned Bruno's wound.

Chapter Eight – Why Grandmother Stormed Out

Bruno's Grandmother was very upset by her son's uniform and what it stood for. She didn't like that Bruno's parents had Hitler over for dinner and she was ashamed at what her son had become. <u>Put yourself in Bruno's Grandmother's shoes</u>. <u>Write a letter</u> from her standpoint to her son (Bruno's father) the day after the Christmas party when she stormed out of Bruno's home. Use the chapter to describe how you feel about him being a commandant, about the new uniform and about how you blame yourself for where he is today.

My Dearest Son,

_____

_____

_____

_____

_____

_____

_____

_____

_____

_____

_____

_____

_____

_____

_____

_____

_____

_____

Love,

Your Mother

Chapter Nine – Bruno Remembers That He Used to Enjoy Exploration

1. Describe Lieutenant Kotler's presence in the home. How did he act around the members of the family?

_____

_____

_____

_____

_____

_____

_____

2. Describe Herr Liszt. How was he different from Bruno's teachers back in Berlin?

_____

_____

_____

3. Why was the history and geography of the Fatherland so important to Herr Liszt?

_____

_____

_____

4. What has Bruno observed about the camp? Name at least 3 things.

_____

_____

_____

_____

Chapter Nine – Bruno Remembers That He Used to Enjoy Exploration

1. Describe Lieutenant Kotler's presence in the home. How did he act around the members of the family?

    a. Treated Bruno like a child.

    b. Acted important and arrogant around Father.

    c. Flirted with Gretel.

    d. Whispered with Mother (implying perhaps improper relations).

    e. Spoke down to the servants and his fellow officers.

2. Describe Herr Liszt. How was he different from Bruno's teachers back in Berlin?

    a. Herr Liszt was a tutor who came to the house every day to give lessons to Bruno and Gretel. He was friendly, but there was anger lingering under the surface. Loved History and Geography. Referred to Bruno as 'young man'.

3. Why was the history and geography of the Fatherland so important to Herr Liszt?

    a. Herr Liszt wanted to teach where Bruno and Gretel came from. He wanted to teach them about how Germany had been wronged in the Treaty of Versailles. The lessons were effective guises for Herr Liszt to teach Nazi doctrines.

4. What has Bruno observed about the camp? Name at least 3 things.

    a. Uniformed soldiers are on the outside.

    b. People with striped pajamas are inside the fence.

    c. Striped pajamas people rarely came to the other side of the fence whereas the guards and even his father went over to their side whenever they pleased.

    d. The guards were clearly in charge.

    e. The guards and his father never seemed to return the courtesy of inviting the people in striped pajamas to the outside.

Chapter Ten – The Dot That Became a Speck That Became a Blob That Became a Figure That Became a Boy

1. According to Bruno, what are the two kinds of discoveries? What category did the boy belong to?

   _____

   _____

   _____

   _____

   _____

   _____

   _____

   _____

2. Draw the star that was on the boy's armband. What do you think this star symbolizes?

   _____

   _____

   _____

   _____

   _____

   _____

3. Bruno explains that Berlin changes when he had lived there. How and why does it change?

   _____

   _____

   _____

   _____

Make a Shmuel Trading Card!

Name: _____

We learn a lot about Shmuel in this chapter. We find a description of what he looks like and even learn when he was born. Gather as much information about Shmuel from this chapter and formulate that information into a trading card. The front will be a picture of Shmuel, and the back box will have his description (i.e. birthdate, nationality, family details, spoken languages, and any other interesting facts).

Front

Back

Chapter Ten – The Dot That Became a Speck That Became a Blob That Became a Figure That Became a Boy

1. According to Bruno, what are the two kinds of discoveries? What category did the boy belong to?

    a. There are interesting things that are just waiting to be discovered – like America.

    b. There are things that are best left alone – like a mouse in the back of the cupboard.

    c. Shmuel belonged to the first category.

2. Draw the star that was on the boy's armband. What do you think this star symbolizes?

✡	This symbol is the star of David.
	It identifies Shmuel as being a Jew, because the star
	is a Jewish symbol.
	Hitler uses the star to identify Jews.

3. Bruno explains that Berlin changes when he had lived there. How and why does it change?

    a. Berlin became very noisy and scary at night. All lights had to be off because of the blackouts. Berlin was being bombed by the Allies in the Second World War.

Chapter Eleven – The Fury

Using a comic strip, summarize the chapter in the boxes below. Use thought or speech bubbles to show dialogue.

Chapter Twelve – Shmuel Thinks of an Answer to Bruno's Question

1. Compare and contrast the two boys' journey to the camp. Make reference to the trains, moving from their homes, the armbands, size of new homes, life at new homes, etc.

Smuel	Bruno

Pick one of the comparisons and illustrate that comparison in the boxes below. For example, if you were to compare the armbands, you could draw a prisoner with the Star of David armband, and a soldier with the swastika armband.

Chapter Twelve – Shmuel Thinks of an Answer to Bruno's Question

1. Compare and contrast the two boys' journey to the camp. Make reference to the trains, moving from their homes, the armbands, size of new homes, life at new homes, etc.

Shmuel	Bruno
• Must wear a Star of David armband • Requisite wearing of armband seen as symbol of oppression and shame.	• Bruno sees soldiers, including his father, wearing armbands with swastikas. Bruno is impressed by the armbands. Seen as a symbol of power and authority.
• Family forced from their home.	• Father chooses to move.
• Nazis/Gestapo came into family's home and initiated the move.	• The Fury/Hitler came into the family's home and initiated the move.
• Made to live in a Ghetto in one room, with other families. Crowded conditions, and Shmuel was hit.	• Family moves to a smaller house – only three floors. Gretel sometimes hit Bruno.
• Train to Auschwitz was crowded and awful.	• Train to new home in Auschwitz was roomy and comfortable
• Shmuel had to walk from the train to the camp.	• Bruno and his family took a car from the train station.
• Shmuel has to work.	• Bruno is bored but gets to explore.
• Shmuel is starving,	• Bruno takes food for granted.

Research ideas:
• Look further into the history of Polish Ghettos, the swastika, Auschwitz, and the Final Solution.
  o Have students give short presentations on one of these items.
  o Hand out research and have students do a think-pair-share.
  o Invite a guest speaker to touch on some of these issues.

Chapter Thirteen – The Bottle of Wine

1. Why did Bruno think that Lieutenant Kotler was a bad soldier but his Father was a good soldier?

_____

_____

_____

_____

_____

_____

2. What did Bruno observe about Pavel?

_____

_____

_____

_____

_____

_____

3. What's Father's belief about History?

_____

_____

_____

_____

_____

4. What does Lieutenant Kotler reveal about his family?

_____

_____

_____

_____

_____

_____

Chapter Thirteen – The Bottle of Wine

1. Why did Bruno think that Lieutenant Kotler was a bad soldier but his Father was a good soldier?
    a. Lieutenant Kotler strides around as if he owns the place, flirts with Gretel and has secrets with Mother.
    b. Father has an impressive uniform, is called Commandant, everyone listens to him, and the Fury has big things in mind for him.
2. What did Bruno observe about Pavel?
    a. Seemed to be getting smaller.
    b. He is getting sadder and thinner.
    c. He has no colour in his face.
    d. His eyes seemed to be filled with tears.
    e. His hands shake.
    f. Pavel seems right out of it – doesn't know what is going on.
3. What's Father's belief about History?
    a. Very important.
    b. Father believes that he and his men were correcting history at Auschwitz by ridding the world of Jews. The war was also seen as a righting of the wrongs of the Treaty of Versailles.
4. What does Lieutenant Kotler reveal about his family?
    a. L. Kotler's father, a professor, left (presumably fled) Germany in the pivotal year of 1938. This was the time when the Nazis were at the peak of power and were mobilising for war. We can assume that he left because of political differences.

Chapter Fourteen – Bruno Tells a Perfectly Reasonable Lie

1. "The grass is greener on the other side of the fence," is a saying about how we view other people's circumstances as better than our own. How is Bruno guilty of this?

   _____

   _____

   _____

   _____

   _____

2. After Bruno slips out Shmuel's name to Gretel, how does he try to cover up his mistake?

   _____

   _____

   _____

   _____

   _____

3. What do you think happened to Shmuel's grandfather?

   _____

   _____

   _____

   _____

Define the following words and write a sentence using your newly defined word.

Trek: (definition) _____

(sentence) _____

Sophistication: (definition) _____

(sentence) _____

Dilemma: (definition) _____

(sentence) _____

Chapter Fourteen – Bruno Tells a Perfectly Reasonable Lie

1. "The grass is greener on the other side of the fence," is a saying about how we view other people's circumstances as better than our own. How is Bruno guilty of this?
    a. Bruno is jealous of the striped pajamas.
    b. Bruno thinks Shmuel has better/more exciting living conditions.
    c. Bruno envies all of the 'friends' Shmuel has on his side of the fence.

2. After Bruno slips out Shmuel's name to Gretel, how does he try to cover up his mistake?
    a. Bruno pretends that he doesn't hear Gretel and simply walks away while whistling to himself.
    b. He finally 'admits' that Shmuel is his imaginary friend.

3. What do you think happened to Shmuel's grandfather?
    a. Shmuel's grandfather has most likely been brought to the gas chamber. The older members of Shmuel's family seem to know that he is no longer alive. We get the impression that Shmuel's father is in mourning.

Chapter Fifteen – Something He Shouldn't Have Done

Think of all the different characters in the story and the connections you can make with them. On the left side, complete the sentence with the name of a character in the story. On the right side, give a brief explanation of how or why you connect, or identity, with that character.

Name of Character:	Explanation
I most admire:	
I mostly dislike:	
I would most likely be a friend to:	
I could learn the most from:	
I would enjoy another book about:	
I would like to know more about:	

Chapter Sixteen – The Haircut

1. Why did Bruno and his family return to Berlin for two days?

_____

_____

_____

2. Why was Father particularly sad?

_____

_____

_____

_____

_____

3. Upon returning to Out-With, what does Bruno realize about the house?

_____

_____

_____

_____

4. What happened to Lieutenant Kotler?

_____

_____

_____

5. Why does Bruno think his friendship with Shmuel is so strange?

_____

_____

_____

_____

_____

6. How has Gretel changed?

_____

_____

_____

_____

_____

7. Why did Bruno get a haircut?

_____

_____

8. What did Mother blame the lice on?

_____

_____

_____

_____

_____

_____

Vocabulary

Use a dictionary to define the following words. After you have defined them, use them in a sentence.

Incident

    Definition: _____

    Sentence: _____

Misshapen

    Definition: _____

    Sentence: _____

Naïve

    Definition: _____

    Sentence: _____

1. Why did Bruno and his family return to Berlin for two days?
    a. Grandmother had died and they returned for the funeral. While there, they stayed in their old house.
2. Why was Father particularly sad?
    a. Father had never made things right with Grandmother after she had 'stormed out'. They had never spoken since that night.
3. Upon returning to Out-With, what does Bruno realize about the house?
    a. Bruno is actually glad to be back. It felt like home. He had missed Shmuel.
4. What happened to Lieutenant Kotler?
    a. Lieutenant Kotler was transferred away.
        i. We can assume that Father sent him away for hiding his past and for getting too close to Mother and maybe even Gretel. We can also assume that we was probably sent to the Eastern Front.
5. Why does Bruno think his friendship with Shmuel is so strange?
    a. All they do is talk together. They have not actually ever played together.
6. How has Gretel changed?
    a. Gretel has put her dolls away and has replaced them with maps with pins. She follows the newspapers and plots the troop movements or victories of the German military.
    b. She know what is happening at Auschwitz and she now believes that the Jews are not real people.
7. Why did Bruno get a haircut?
    a. Bruno gets lice.
8. What did Mother blame the lice on?
    a. "It's the filth around here that did it. If some people could only see the effect this place is having on us all."

Chapter Seventeen – Mother Gets Her Own Way

1. How does Bruno feel about the prospect of going back to Berlin?

_____

_____

_____

_____

_____

_____

_____

2. What do we learn about Bruno's mother? Why is Bruno concerned about her?

_____

_____

_____

_____

_____

_____

_____

3. What made Father sure he had made the right decision in planning to send Mother, Gretel, and Bruno back to Berlin?

_____

_____

_____

_____

_____

Chapter Seventeen – Mother Gets Her Own Way

1. How does Bruno feel about the prospect of going back to Berlin?
    a. Bruno didn't know what to think – so many things had changed.
    b. He couldn't remember who his Berlin friends had been.
    c. Grandmother was dead.
    d. Grandfather was senile.
    e. He didn't mind Herr Liszt anymore.
    f. Had a better/friendlier relationship with Maria than back in Berlin.
    g. Gretel was not quite so hopeless.
    h. Shmuel was here.

2. What do we learn about Bruno's mother? Why is Bruno concerned about her?
    a. She was spending all day in bed.
    b. She doesn't talk to Father.
    c. She is drinking 'medicinal sherries'.

3. What made Father sure he had made the right decision in planning to send Mother, Gretel, and Bruno back to Berlin?
    a. After Bruno slips about the children he sees, Father realizes that Bruno and Gretel have seen too much. Father sees that Bruno's innocence cannot be protected at Auschwitz.

Chapter Eighteen – Thinking Up the Final Adventure

1. What concern did Shmuel share with Bruno?

_____

_____

_____

_____

_____

2. What did Shmuel and Bruno regret about all the time they spent together?

_____

_____

_____

_____

_____

3. What was the *Final Adventure*?

_____

_____

_____

_____

_____

4. Make a prediction about how the 'final adventure' turns out.

_____

_____

_____

_____

_____

_____

☞ Research the "Final Solution". Write down some of the key ideas and facts about this part of the setting of *The Boy in the Striped Pajamas*.

Chapter Eighteen – Thinking Up the Final Adventure

1. What concern did Shmuel share with Bruno?
    a. Shmuel could not find his father. He had left for a work duty and none of the men came back. We can assume that the work party were executed or marched to the gas chambers.

2. What did Shmuel and Bruno regret about all the time they spent together?
    a. They never got to play together. Bruno regrets that he had never been to Shmuel's side of the fence.

3. What was the *Final Adventure*?
    a. Bruno was going to don striped pajamas and wriggle underneath the fence to join Shmuel. Together they would explore and try to find Shmuel's father.

Chapter Nineteen – What Happened the Next Day

1. Why do you think the author has included the detail about the rainy, stormy weather?

_____

_____

_____

_____

2. What is Bruno reminded of when he puts on the striped pajamas? Why do you think this is significant? What does this tell us about Bruno?

_____

_____

_____

_____

_____

_____

_____

_____

3. What happens to Shmuel and Bruno?

_____

_____

_____

_____

_____

_____

_____

4. In the boxes below, draw a picture of what Bruno thought the camp would look like inside, and what he really saw. Use the descriptions found in this chapter.

What he *thought* the camp would look like:

What he actually saw:

Chapter Nineteen – What Happened the Next Day

1. Why do you think the author has included the detail about the rainy, stormy weather?

    a. This sets the mood – sombre and serious.

    b. The storm foreshadows something ominous or troubling.

    c. Bruno's boots are getting stuck in the mud, almost as if nature itself is telling Bruno to stop and turn back.

2. What is Bruno reminded of when he puts on the striped pajamas? Why do you think this is significant? What does this tell us about Bruno?

    a. Bruno is reminded of Grandmother and the plays they used to put on for the family. He had always enjoyed getting into character and dressing up in costumes.

    b. This memory shows Bruno's innocence and naivety. He thinks he is still in some kind of play or is dressing up. He doesn't see the dreadful reality around him.

3. What happens to Shmuel and Bruno?

    a. They get rounded up and marched to a gas chamber while trying to find Shmuel's father.

    b. Bruno thinks they are brought inside to get away from the rain, but they are led into a gas chamber.

    c. *Their final adventure becomes part of the final solution.*

Chapter Twenty – The Last Chapter

1. How does Father connect the dots about Bruno's disappearance?

_____

_____

_____

_____

_____

_____

2. What becomes of Father?

_____

_____

_____

_____

_____

_____

3. "Of course all this happened a long time ago and nothing like that could ever happen again. Not in this day and age." What do you think the author is trying to say? Does he really believe this?

_____

_____

_____

_____

_____

_____

Chapter Twenty – The Last Chapter

1. How does Father connect the dots about Bruno's disappearance?
   a. Father connects Bruno's discarded clothes by the spot in the fence where the fencing could be lifted up. He knows Bruno went in the camp and was swept up in one of the extermination sweeps.
2. What becomes of Father?
   a. Father gets captured by the Allies when the camp is liberated. He loses the will to live after he realizes that Bruno had been caught up in the Auschwitz death machine.
3. "Of course all this happened a long time ago and nothing like that could ever happen again. Not in this day and age." What do you think the author is trying to say? Does he really believe this?

Evaluate the Story...

Discussion questions:

- Do you think this is a realistic story?

- Do you think Bruno could really be so naïve?

- If what Father was doing was right (in his eyes), why was he so careful to protect Bruno from the truth about what was happening in Auschwitz?

- How do you feel about the ending of the book?

- If you were the author, how would you have ended the book?

- In what ways did the horror of the camp seep into the house?

- Has there been anything comparable to the Holocaust since WWII?

- How can something as evil as the 'Final Solution' be allowed to happen?

- Why did people like Bruno's father go along so willingly with Hitler's plan of extermination?

- Herr Liszt was in the process of indoctrinating or brainwashing Bruno and Gretel into accepting Nazi belief. Who indoctrinated Herr Liszt? In other words, where did these evil ideas first come from?

- How is it possible for people to be so cruel? What is the antidote to cruelty?

- Show how 'innocence' is a theme in *The Boy in the Striped Pajamas*.

Other books by Greg Slingerland:

A Teacher's Guide to The Hobbit

A Teacher's Guide to I Am David

A Teacher's Guide to A Christmas Carol

A Teacher's Guide to The Joy Luck Club

Printed in Great Britain
by Amazon